Psalm 23

Illustrated Ros Webb

Psalm 23

Illustrated by Ros Webb

I will praise You, for I am fearfully and wonderfully made; Marvelous are Your works, And that my soul knows very well. Psalm 139-14

The Lord is my shepherd;
I shall not want.

He maketh me to lie down in green pastures:

He leadeth me
beside the still waters.

He restoreth my soul:

Thou preparest
a table before me
in the presence of
mine enemies

Thou anointest my head with oil

My cup runneth over

Surely goodness and mercy shall follow me all the days of my life

And I will dwell
in the house of
the Lord forever.

About the illustrator

Ros Webb has been illustrating and writing children's books for over a decade. Collaborating with hundreds of different authors, Ros has co-produced a selection of inspiring and imaginative children's picture books.

Her style has been described as fun, bright, and whimsical and her work always brings a smile.

Ros started out as a self-published author/illustrator with her story "The Big Sleepy Bear and the Pink Flamingos" and has gone on to self-publish a selection of other books.

Ros works with authors from across the globe and is continually inspired by their imagination and story telling ability.

contact us Facebook
https://www.facebook.
com/TheChildrensBookIllustrator

Printed in Great Britain
by Amazon